Life Cycles of Living Things

Amphibian Life Cycle

Tracy Vonder Brink

Table of Contents

A Starfish Book

SEAHORSE PUBLISHING

Teaching Tips for Caregivers:

As a caregiver, you can help your child succeed in school by giving them a strong foundation in language and literacy skills and a desire to learn to read.

This book helps children grow by letting them practice reading skills.

Reading for pleasure and interest will help your child to develop reading skills and will give your child the opportunity to practice these skills in meaningful ways.

- Encourage your child to read on her own at home
- Encourage your child to practice reading aloud
- Encourage activities that require reading
- Establish a reading time
- Talk with your child
- Give your child writing materials

Teaching Tips for Teachers:

Research shows that one of the best ways for students to learn a new topic is to read about it.

Before Reading

- Read the "Words to Know" and discuss the meaning of each word.
- Read the back cover to see what the book is about.

During Reading

- When a student gets to a word that is unknown, ask them to look at the rest of the sentence to find clues to help with the meaning of the unknown word.
- Ask the student to write down any pages of the book that were confusing to them.

After Reading

- Discuss the main idea of the book.
- Ask students to give one detail that they learned in the book by showing a text dependent answer from the book.

Amphibian Life Cycle

All living things are born.

They grow to be adults.

We call these changes a life cycle.

Amphibians are animals with backbones.

They live part of their lives in water and part on land.

Amphibians are **cold-blooded**.

Amphibians also have smooth skin.

An amphibian's life cycle begins with an egg.

An **embryo** grows inside.

Most amphibians lay their eggs in water.

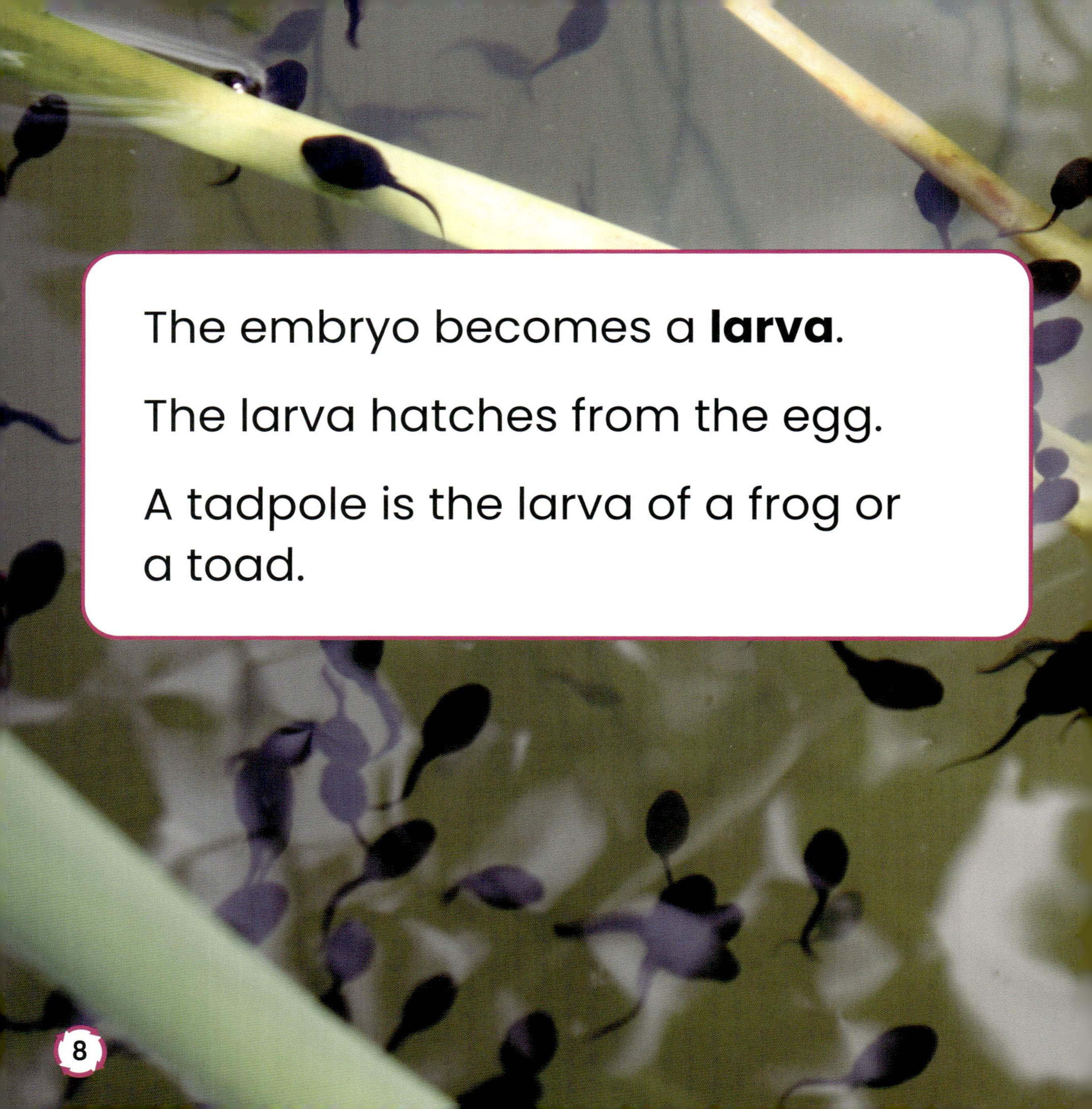

The embryo becomes a **larva**.

The larva hatches from the egg.

A tadpole is the larva of a frog or a toad.

A tadpole lives in water.

It has a tail.

It breathes underwater through **gills**.

A tadpole grows legs.

It grows **lungs** to breathe air.

We call these big changes a **metamorphosis**.

Salamanders do not lose their tails during metamorphosis.

Salamanders are amphibians like frogs and toads.

Salamanders also go through metamorphosis.

Amphibians can leave the water after they grow legs and lungs.

They are able to live on land.

The skin on a frog's throat puffs out to make his call louder.

Adult amphibians find mates.

Some males call to females.

The females look for the loudest male.

The females lay eggs.

The life cycle begins again.

Words to Know

cold-blooded (kohld BLUHD-id): unable to make body heat; having a body temperature that changes with the temperature of the surroundings

embryo (EM-bree-oh): a living creature in the earliest stage of development, before it is hatched or born

gills (gilz): body parts near the mouth in fish and other living creatures that allow them to breathe underwater

larva (LAHR-vuh): a stage in the development of many living creatures that happens between birth or hatching and before adulthood

lungs (luhngz): body parts that people and some animals use to breathe air

metamorphosis (met-uh-MOR-fuh-sis): a major change in the form and appearance of some living creatures that happens as they become adults